# We Live in Boise

WRITTEN BY
*Elisabeth McKetta & James Stead*

ILLUSTRATED BY
*April VanDeGrift*

frog prince press
stories that change people

I live in Boise, a city that runs into the hills. Here, wild sage grows and foxes dart just out of sight. When I was a baby my father carried me into the foothills wrapped in his coat. The wind blew and the snow flaked and I slept and slept, all through the bright cold winter.

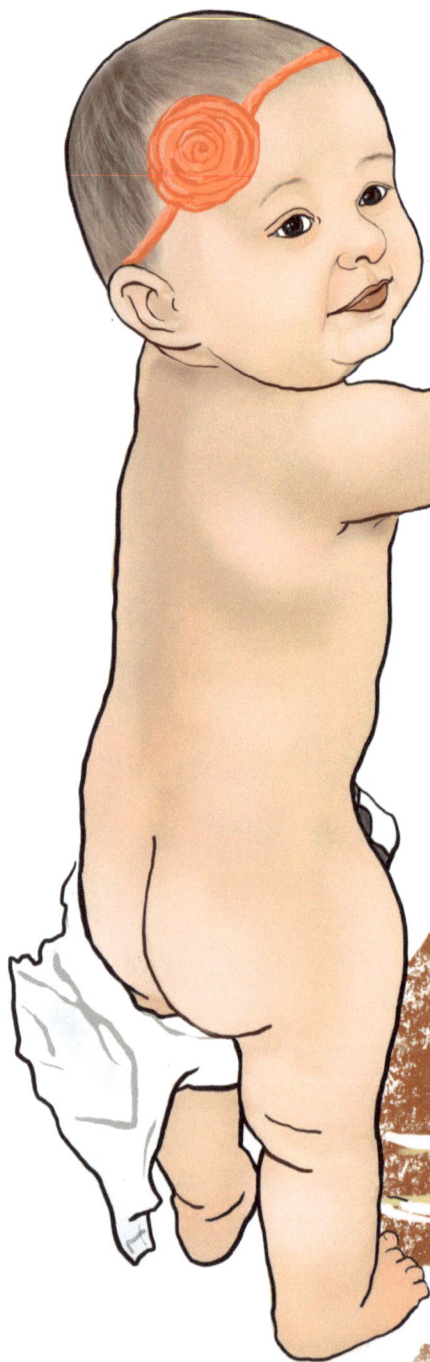

I live in Boise, a city that loves an outdoor party. In the Grove Plaza downtown, bands play concerts long into the night. When I was one, I danced in the fountain at the plaza and got sopping wet. I danced so much that my diaper started to fall off.

I live in Boise, a generous city. I know a woman named Rainbow who gives away balloon animals at the farmer's market. When I was two, I asked for a dog for myself and a fishing pole for my sister. My sister's balloon popped before we even left the market.

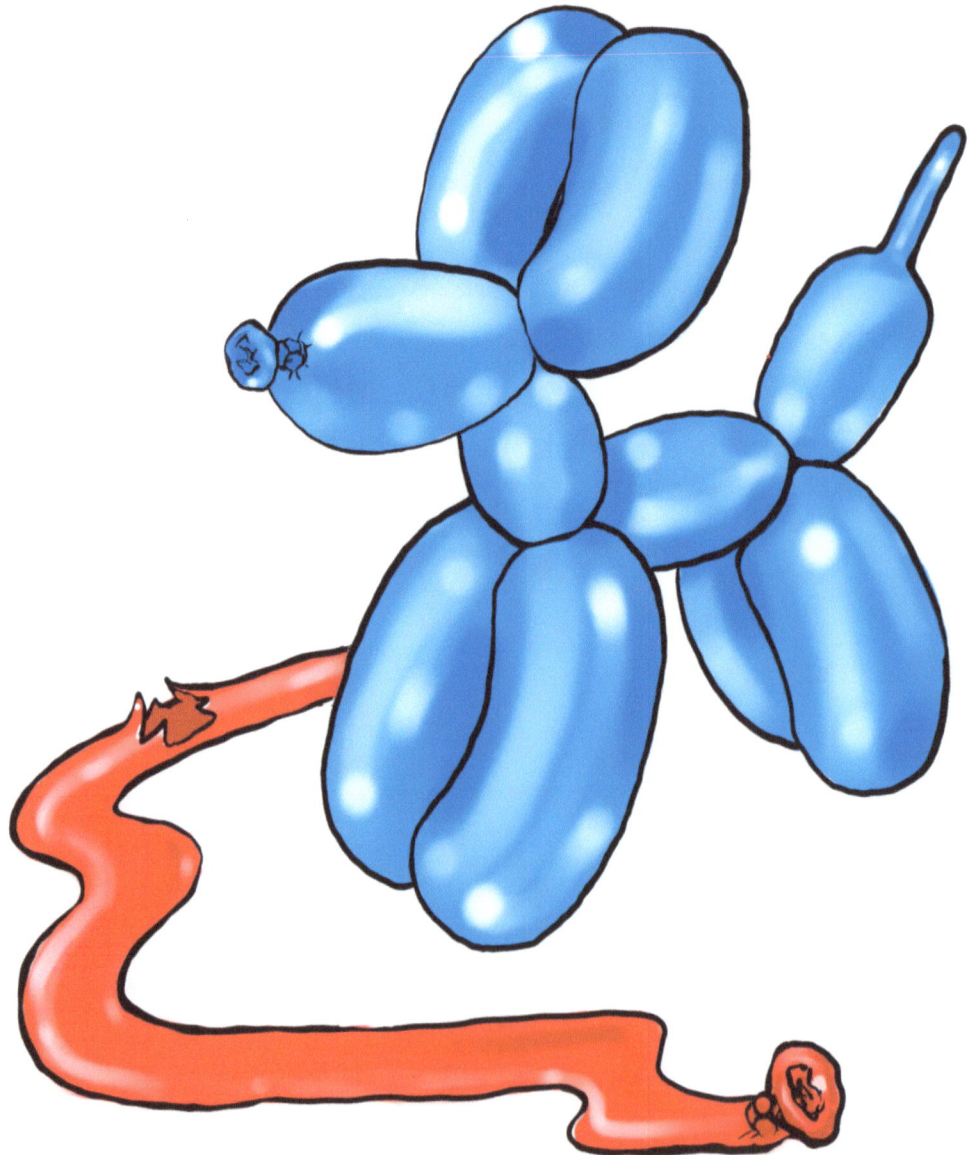

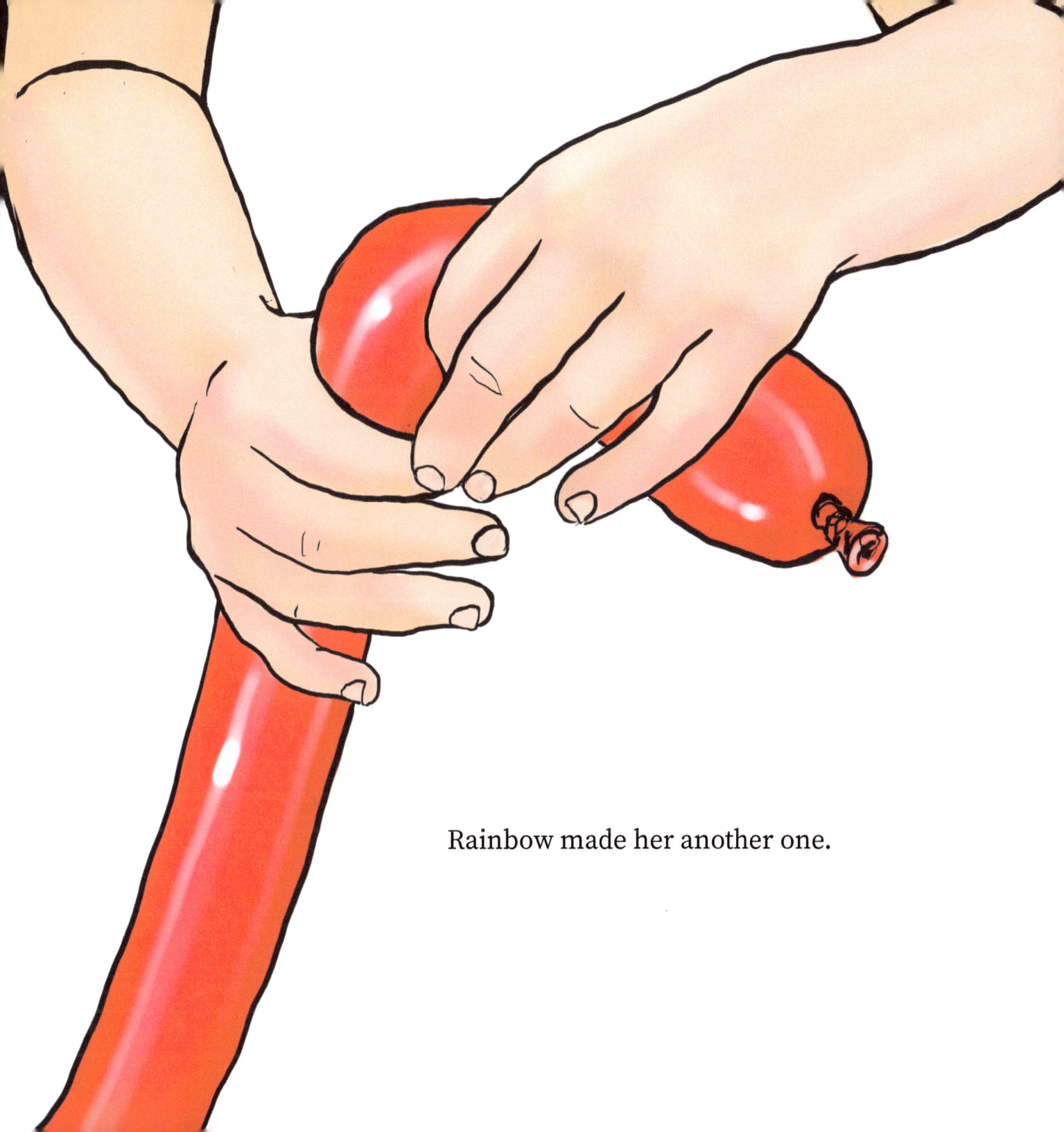

Rainbow made her another one.

I live in Boise, a city that preserves its past. The Boise Depot is an old train station, but I've never seen a train there. My grandpa said he once took a train called the *Portland Rose* from Boise to Chicago. When I was three, we had a picnic at the Depot and I wore my engineer cap.

I live in Boise, a city that appreciates art. In Freak Alley, artists paint words and ants and mermaids, and once a year they wash the walls and the artists begin all over. When I was four, one of the artists handed me his paintbrush and I helped fill in the waves of an ocean.

I live in Boise, a city that cares about animals. Zoo Boise was the first in the country to dedicate a portion of their admissions fee to conservation, so every time we go, we are helping save elephants, lions, and hippos in Africa. When I was five, I saw a mother monkey swing from a branch holding her baby in one arm. I asked my mom if she would try that with me.

"We'll see," she said.

I live in Boise, a city that welcomes refugees, people who must leave their own homes in countries far away. Thousands of people have come to Boise as refugees and they speak many languages. When I was six, I met my best friend, who is from Syria—she taught me how to say "Ahabek," which means "I love you."

I showed her how to go backward on the monkey bars.

I live in Boise, a city that loves to bike. Our Greenbelt runs thirty miles past the parks people call the Ribbon of Jewels, each one named after a famous Boise woman. My favorite is called Kristin Armstrong Municipal Park. Kristin is a mom who lives in Boise and she's one of the fastest cyclists in the world. When I was seven she won the gold medal and her child asked, "Mama, why are you crying? You won!"

"Sometimes we cry when we are happy," she said.

I live in Boise, a city that gardens. Deer wander our neighborhoods and taste our plants. One spring a very old elk moved into our community garden and we called her Ada and brought her apples. When I was eight, I fed Ada lettuce that I had grown myself. After she was gone, we made t-shirts with her picture on it and threw her a goodbye party.

I live in Boise, a city that looks up into the sky. At Spirit of Boise, hot air balloons rise like bubbles from the wet park grass.

When I was nine, one balloon landed in our neighbor's yard, and her dog came out to greet it. I hope they land in my yard next year.

I live in Boise, a city that supports the home team. Every fall, thousands of people pour into the college stadium to watch football. When I was ten, I saw my cousin play on the blue turf, and we sat high in the stands, cheering our heads off and shivering under a blanket. The Broncos won the game.

I live in Boise, a city that is rich with snow. When the branches are bare, we pack our skis and drive up the twisty road to our mountain, Bogus Basin. When I was eleven, I competed in my first ski race, and I grinned the whole way down.

I live in Boise, a city surrounded by rivers where people raft. In the summer, the Boise River gushes over rocks and we float in tubes to cool off. Sometimes my mom dives in and we think she's crazy, because even in the summer the water is freezing. When I was twelve, I helped guide a raft down the Payette River and knew the names of all the rapids.

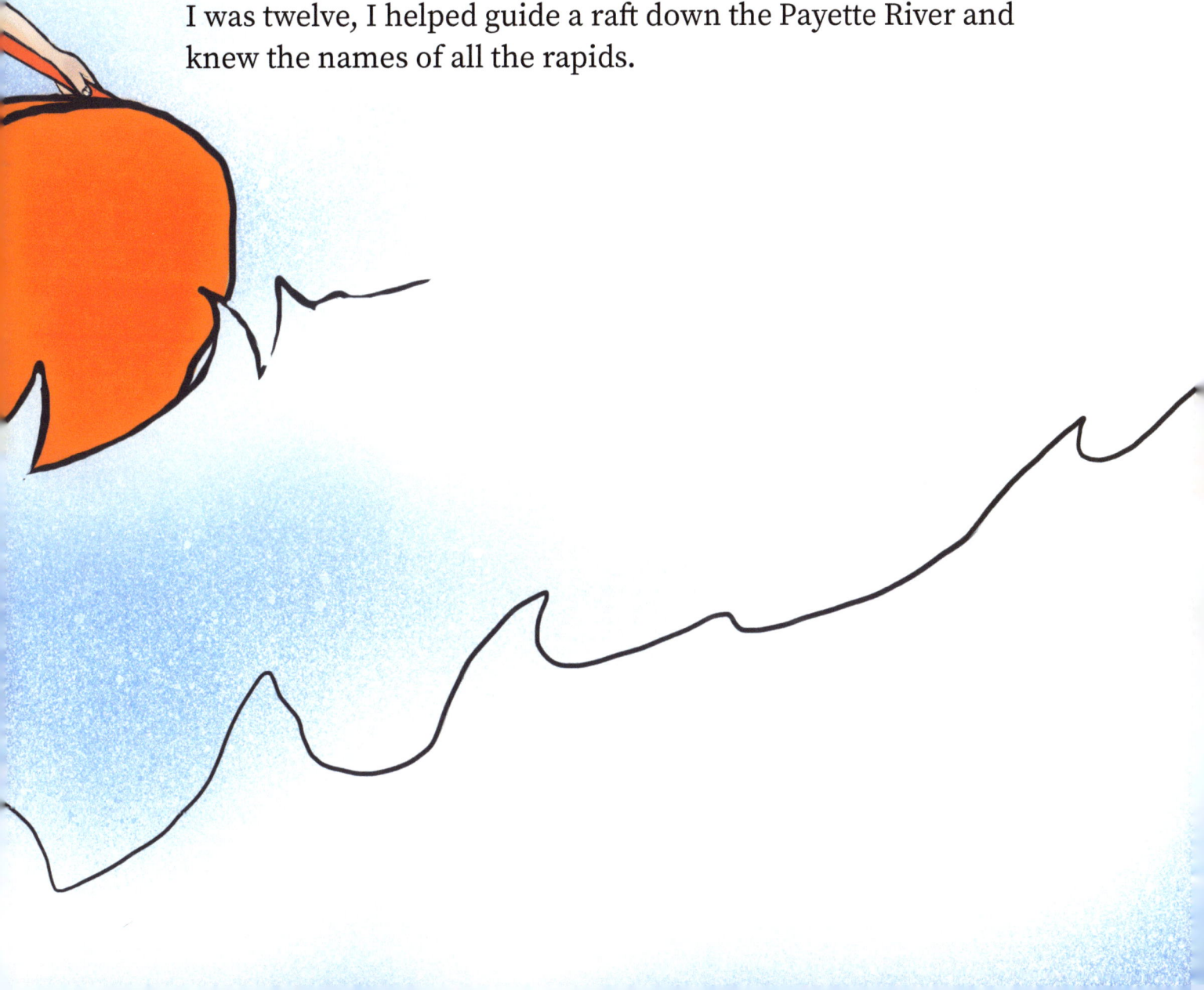

I live in Boise, a musical city. Once a year we have Treefort, and people come from all over and the downtown swells overnight. When I was thirteen, I got a ticket to the main stage show and danced for hours with my friends. I saw my English teacher, who was dancing too, and I felt sure that in my city grownups can have as much fun as kids.

We live in Boise, a city that was small and now is growing. Cranes rise in the skyline and backhoes turn up the dirt. Just like our city, we have grown up too, and now we have our own babies. From our windows, we can see the foothills, just as they've always been.

*Dedicated to our children—*
*Snowden, Olson, Zoe, Oliver, and Finn—*
*and all of Boise's children.*

Photo by Paige McLeod

**Elisabeth McKetta** lives in Boise, where she writes, teaches, hikes in the foothills, and adventures around town with James Stead and their two kids.

**James Stead** lives in Boise, where he mountain bikes, swims, sells real estate, eats tacos, and adventures around town with Elisabeth McKetta and their two kids.

**April VanDeGrift** is an artist, illustrator, adjunct professor, and mother of three from Boise, Idaho.

Frog Prince Press
www.frogprincepress.com
Boise, Idaho

Copyright © 2019 Elisabeth Sharp McKetta and James Stead

ISBN: 978-0-9908323-5-5

Illustrations by April VanDeGrift, layout by Sarah Tregay

www.ingramcontent.com/pod-product-compliance
Lightning Source LLC
Chambersburg PA
CBHW042009090426
42811CB00015B/1590